Granny Butterfly's Birthday

 This is the SECOND in a series of 'Illustrated Children's Books about Granny Butterfly (a Red Admiral) and her butterfly friends and family.

In book ONE Bertrum (a Clouded Yellow) decides it's time to leave the safety of 'Honeysuckle Meadow' and venture out into the unknown, with mishaps on the way.

In this SECOND book Bertrum decides to take his friend Boris on an adventure, but gets himself into many more mishaps!!!!

 A charming book that will educate children in identifying different species of Butterfly.

Which Butterfly would your child like to be?

Written by Jean French
Illustrated by Brian Marriott

Grosvenor House
Publishing Limited

All rights reserved
Copyright © Jean French, 2017

The right of Jean French to be identified as the author of this
work has been asserted in accordance with Section 78
of the Copyright, Designs and Patents Act 1988

The book cover picture is copyright to Jean French

This book is published by
Grosvenor House Publishing Ltd
Link House
140 The Broadway, Tolworth, Surrey, KT6 7HT.
www.grosvenorhousepublishing.co.uk

This book is sold subject to the conditions that it shall not, by way of
trade or otherwise, be lent, resold, hired out or otherwise circulated
without the author's or publisher's prior consent in any form of binding or
cover other than that in which it is published and
without a similar condition including this condition being imposed
on the subsequent purchaser.

A CIP record for this book
is available from the British Library

ISBN 978-1-78623-258-8

Dedicated to my late mother, Evelyn.

"Before she died, she always said that when she did, she would come back as a butterfly. So when my children, grandchildren and great-grandchildren visit her grave they always say "We are going to see Granny Butterfly". This is what inspired me to write a children's book with this title."

On a recent Caribbean cruise, Jean had completed her gym workout and went to pick up her water bottle only to find a butterfly had landed there. In the middle of an ocean?! She gently returned to her cabin with the butterfly still attached to the bottle. Jean very much a 'spiritual person' believes this was a sign from her mother.

Jean French was born in Stanhill Village, Lancashire and lived in Kent, Nottinghamshire, Cambridgeshire before moving to the Isle of Wight in 1975. It is on the Island that she met and married her husband, Roger, in 1982.

Jean and Roger live on the Island with their family of five children, eleven grandchildren, and three great grandchildren.

Granny Butterfly, who is a [Red Admiral Butterfly](), is very special to all the other Butterflies as she was the first Butterfly to discover Honeysuckle Meadow and that it is such a magical place to live, as everyone that lives there are completely safe and live for a very long time.

Bertrum, who is a [Clouded Yellow Butterfly](), is adventurous and likes doing things he is not supposed to do. That is why he is the first butterfly to leave Honeysuckle Meadow for an adventure.

Boris, who is a [Purple Emperor Butterfly](), is rather clumsy and gets into a lot of trouble.

Today is Granny Butterfly's Birthday. Nobody really knows how old she is, as she has lived for a very long time. She was the first butterfly to discover Honeysuckle Meadow and its unexpected magical qualities.

It is such a charming place to live, as everyone that lives there, lives for a very long time, and they are completely safe.

All of her friends and family are there to celebrate her birthday and they are all having a wonderful time.

It's a beautiful summer's day, not a cloud in the sky, so everybody is flapping their wings with happiness.

All the flowers in the meadow are in full bloom, so there's plenty to eat and drink. The baby butterflies are chasing each other in and out of the hedgerows and even Bertrum is enjoying himself.

He still remembers the dangerous, yet wonderful, adventure he had on that fateful day. But also that he nearly didn't make it back home!

He knows that the next time he has an adventure, he has to be more careful, and that is why he has decided he must take a friend with him.

The difficult decision Bertrum has to make is which one? Going through his list of friends, he thinks who would be best:

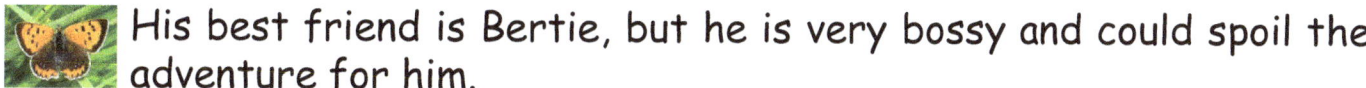 His best friend is Bertie, but he is very bossy and could spoil the adventure for him.

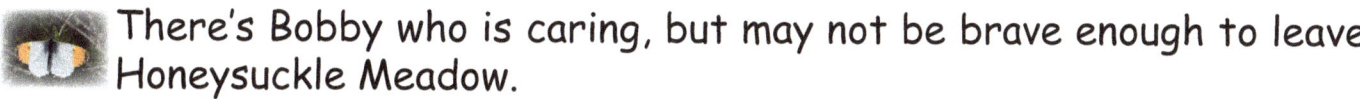 There's Bobby who is caring, but may not be brave enough to leave Honeysuckle Meadow.

 Beatrice, kind and helpful?

 Bella, full of her own importance. No!! Definitely not her!!

 Betsy, sweet and tiny. Hmmm... not sure.

 Boris, clumsy. Now he would be a laugh, but would he get us into more trouble?

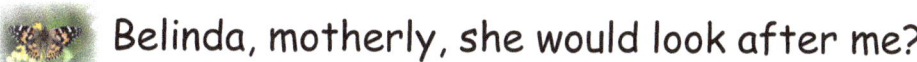 Barnaby, easily distracted, maybe he would be ok?

Basil, the only thing he eats is Basil. Nice butterfly, but a bit of a nightmare!!

Belinda, motherly, she would look after me?

Bluebell, forgetful, even gets lost in Bluebell Woods, **don't think so!!**

As Bertrum doesn't need to make a decision straight away, he decides to think long and hard before making his mind up.

Several days pass and everyone is enjoying the lovely weather. This is what prompts Bertrum into thinking that now would be the perfect time to go exploring.

He has decided that he is going to ask Boris, because whatever happens he knows he will have a lot of fun if he comes along and it won't be boring.

He flies over to him and asks him if he is ready for a bit of excitement. At first Boris isn't sure what he means, so Bertrum tells him all the things that happened on his last adventure, and that he is ready for a new one.

Bertrum has decided that the next time he goes he should fly in the opposite direction from Honeysuckle Meadow as he still remembers what happened when the big giant butterfly tried to catch him. So as he doesn't want that happening again, the safest plan will be to avoid going in that direction from now on.

Boris also knows that he is not allowed to leave Honeysuckle Meadow, as like Bertrum, Granny Butterfly has told him several times that it is not safe to do so.

But after what Bertrum has just told him, he can't help himself; the excitement is too great, so he is willing to take the risk and can't wait to get going.

Bertrum and Boris have decided that the best time to go would be the next time Granny Butterfly takes them to Bluebell Woods, because no one will see them take off, as they will be too busy enjoying themselves.

Whenever they go, they know that it is very important to have a good breakfast before they leave, or they will not have enough energy for the flight.

Bertrum will never forget what happened the last time, when he just took off without thinking or having something to eat. This time it will be different, besides Granny Butterfly is always telling them that breakfast is the most important meal of the day.

As Butterflies, Bertrum and Boris are totally different characters, but still get on really well and are very good friends.

Bertrum is a clouded yellow, smaller and quick flying.

Where as Boris being a Purple Emperor is much bigger and very clumsy, flying into things without looking where he is going.

Granny Butterfly has just announced that the next day she is taking everyone to Bluebell Woods, so early to bed tonight, as they will have an early start tomorrow. Then they can have a good long day, enjoying themselves in their favourite place.

Bertrum and Boris can hardly sleep with the thought of what lies ahead, and the new adventures they are going to have.

Before they know it, morning has come and everyone is awake and having their breakfast, Bertrum and Boris are filling themselves up with Heather, Buddleia and their favourite meal Thistle. Making sure that they have eaten enough to give them all the energy they will need when they take off.

Granny Butterfly gets everyone together to fly next door to Bluebell Woods. She knows by doing this, nobody will get lost.

Bertrum and Boris take off with all the other butterflies and land in Bluebell Woods, they then start to make for the far corner and wait for the right opportunity to fly over the hedgerows for their big adventure.

Suddenly, coming around the corner, close to Bluebell Woods is a red and white open top bus. This is their perfect chance to go. They quickly fly over the hedgerows and land on the top deck of the bus, to see which direction the bus is going.

Luckily, the bus is going away from the sea, so Bertrum is happy, he doesn't want them to have the problem with the big giant butterfly again.

What Bertrum doesn't know is that he lives on an Island called 'Mariposa', so no matter which direction, he takes, he will always be close to the sea.

After a short time, the red and white open top bus goes into a field where there is a Village Fair, with stalls selling lots of lovely things to eat including Candy Floss.

Boris loves the smell and as he is always hungry, he can't resist flying down to taste one that has fallen to the ground.

He lands smack in the middle and when he tries to lift his legs he soon realises that he is completely stuck. Bertrum can't believe it.

They have only just started their adventure and already there is a problem. How is he going to get his friend free of this sweet sticky mess?

An old lady passing by sees what has happened, and lifts the stick of the candy floss into the air and waves it about. All of a sudden Boris is free.

Thank goodness for that thinks Bertrum, but he is not happy that Boris has ignored his instructions and gone off on his own.

All the villagers are having a wonderful time with many things to do including Donkey rides, Egg and Spoon races, sack race, three legged race and lots, lots more; with stalls all around the field.

After Boris has licked himself clean, the friends decide to take a look around and see if there is anything safe to do.

As they fly around the field, they see some groups of children waiting to have a donkey ride.

Boris is overcome with excitement and without thinking flies over to where the donkeys are standing and lands smack in the middle of one of their heads.

With that the poor, startled donkey takes off, galloping around the field with his owner running behind trying to catch him.

In the mean time, Boris is having a wonderful time, unaware of the trouble he has caused.

By now Bertrum is getting really fed up with Boris, but this is only the beginning, as Boris is soon bored with having a donkey ride and decides he would prefer to be in an egg and spoon race instead.

All the children are lined up to start the race, as the whistle goes, they start to run, but as they do Boris flies up from one spoon to another, having a great time, but the children are so surprised to see a beautiful butterfly land on their spoons, that they stop running and drop their eggs, which is the perfect time for Boris to take off and find something more exciting to do.

He sees two teams of men pulling on a rope and flies down to have a closer look, now that could be good fun he thinks, and decides to help by landing on the man in front, whose team is just about to win the tug of war game.

The man is so astonished to see a Purple Emperor butterfly land on his hands that he accidently lets go of the rope and the other team win the prize instead.

Well, that wasn't as much fun as I thought, thinks Boris, so flies off to see if there is something more exciting to do.

As he does, he notices in the far corner of the field, a large tent where there is a cake competition being held.

As Boris flies over he sees all the beautiful cakes on display and flies down for a closer look. Just as he is about to land on the biggest cake, someone sees him and shouts :

"STOP THAT BUTTERFLY before he can do any more damage!"

While all this is going on Bertrum is at the other side of the field and is getting really worried and upset about his missing friend, he has looked everywhere for him and is just about to give up hope, when he sees everyone running towards a large tent in the corner of the field.

He knows that if there is a problem there, then that is where he will find Boris.

He quickly flies over to see what is happening and there are lots of people shouting and running all over the place with their hands in the air and in the centre of all the chaos is Boris.

OH NO! What has he done **now**, thinks Bertrum. But whatever it is, I have got to help him, so he flies over to his friend and shouts,

"Quickly! Follow me." Boris being big and clumsy can't fly as fast as Bertrum, but he knows he has to keep up with his friend if he wants to escape and get home safe. They make for the entrance of the tent and luckily before anyone can stop them, they are out and flying high into the sky.

Bertrum knows his way home, as he remembered in which direction the red and white open top bus was taking on the way to the village fair. So it is not long before they see Bluebell Woods ahead of them, and land safely in one of the trees.

Both Bertrum and Boris are completely exhausted and glad when Granny Butterfly gathers everyone together to fly home to Honeysuckle Meadow.

Bertrum has decided as soon as they are home and settled, he is going to have a few words to say to Boris and one of them is, that apart from causing havoc wherever he went, he spoiled his day out because he spent all of his time looking after him, and not having an adventure of his own, and definitely, the next time he goes, he is going to take someone with him who is less trouble than him.

Boris is very sorry that his friend is cross with him and he knows that if he hadn't invited him along he wouldn't have had such a wonderful adventure.

So he flies over to where Bertrum is and says "Thank you so much for a wonderful day. You are my very special friend and the next time we go off together, I promise to be <u>very good</u>."

Bertrum can't stay cross with his friend for long so as they settle down in the long grass for the night, he thinks to himself ….. "today wasn't just about me, it was for giving my unique friend Boris a special treat and for making him happy, as he makes me (sometimes!)"